Long Feud

LONG FEUD | *Selected Poems*

by | LOUIS UNTERMEYER

HARCOURT, BRACE & WORLD, INC. | *New York*

8 1 1
U

Note | The poems in this collection consist of a selection from previously published volumes, together with later poems. They are the only ones I care to preserve. Since no one but a researcher is interested in dates of composition, the titles are arranged alphabetically rather than chronologically.

The poems "Arctic Agrarian," "Jerusalem Delivered," "Upon Washington Bridge," and "'In the Beginning . . .'" appeared originally in *The New Yorker*. "A Displaced Orpheus" was the Phi Beta Kappa poem read at Harvard in 1955 and published in *The Atlantic Monthly* in September 1955.   L. U.

Contents

"Breathe! Move again! Awake! Break through
This long pretense of sleep! Weep low
Or laugh, or merely feign to smile.
Whisper small words like 'love' and 'you,'
But stir and come to life again.
Say something, anything. Or listen while
I sing you out of silence, out of pain. . . ."

He stopped. No use. He'd said it all before.
Probably better. He had lost the knack
Of making the dead bones of speech cry out,
Shaking the mind with unaccustomed words,
Innocent and clairvoyant. . . . He was through.

There was a time when everything stood still
To hear his lightest grace note. Howling beasts
Gathered around on tiptoe; prowling lions
Forswearing fierceness, purred their ecstasy.
The hen, dreaming of eagles, preened herself
And nestled closer to the enraptured fox.
The tyrant vulture and the timid wren
Pressed wing to wing in worship. Nightingales
Improved their coloratura. Tropic trees
And mountaintops that freeze bowed themselves.
Even the billows shouting from the sea
Hung their great heads in an adoring hush.

But that was long ago. Now all was changed.
The mountains sat in stony unconcern.
The waves had business of their own. The beasts
Had casually deserted him and, worse,
Had all turned critics, while the birds
Were screaming birds of prey. He could not charm
The hungriest sparrow from the nearest bush.
The virtue had gone out of him. . . . And yet . . .
There must be ways of winning back again

That magic sleight-of-tongue, the trick of song:
The feet that danced and beat in balanced time,
With all the little echoing bells of rhyme. . . .
There must be ways. And he would learn them all;
Learn—by the book—what once he knew by heart;
Learn by example, theory, and rule,
Whatever modern poetry could impart. . . .

And so he came to earth, and went to school.

The first course he encountered was a class
In cold anxiety, where sentiment
Had been exchanged for sensibility,
And personal emotion had become
Impersonal detachment. It was chic
To be unmoved, acute and clinical,
To be an oracle as well as wit,
Coupling minute precisions out of Pope
With soft-shoe patter straight from vaudeville.
Here the disciples of the modern Muse,
Aggressive children from progressive schools,
Learned how to take a flat banality
And make it sound as baleful as a bomb,
Twisting the ordinary turn of speech
With extra-audenary menace. . . . So,
Having observed how it was done, he changed
His pitch and hopefully rephrased his song.

"The breakfast lurks on the table,
        The tea conspires in the cup,
The nightmare screams from the headlines,
        Get up, my pet, get up.

"Happy and whole in his Homburg,
        The minister hatches his crime;
The fall-out drifts over Greenland,
        It's time, my pet, it's time.

"Dripping with ermine and emeralds,
    The Truth knows nothing but lies;
Virtue is anyone's call-girl,
        Open, my pet, your eyes.

"The saint seduces the sinner,
    While Eve is instructing the snake.
Love ends in a vicious *fermata*.
        Awake, poor fool, awake.

"Where Midas murders his mistress
    In the house that was built by jack,
Mary has lamb for her luncheon,
        And pure Snow White is black.

"If hate can be radiant with reason,
    And war is a *sine qua non*,
If evil's not simply enchanting,
        Sleep on, my pet, sleep on."

No! No! The tune was thin, the tone was false.
The words betrayed his meaning out of shape,
Reducing love to mordant flippancies
And leering fairy tales. It would not do.
He wandered on. . . . He found another school . . .
Established in the ruins; here the rats
Nested in hollow statues. Pan and his nymphs
Coupled among tin cans and rusted springs.
Half sordid and half sacrosanct, it was
A school where common sense surrendered to
A dark, uncommon sense of suffering,
Where flagellated flesh not only craved
The anguish of the bone but, mourned by ants,
The slow attrition of the skeleton.
Here words and feelings struggled to attain
Delicate imprecisions of nuance;
Here time and timelessness together stood
At the still center of a wasted world,

3

Yearning toward death. . . . Once more he tried to learn
A newer tone, another attitude.
And thus, in a defunctive sermon, spoke:

    "Between the concept and the execution,
    After the end, before the beginning,
    Between the sinning and the suffering,
        Open your dead eyes.

    "Between the doubts and indecisions,
    Among the small poetic agonies—
    Aus meinen grossen Schmerzen
    Mach ich die kleinen Lieder—
    You will confront Priapus at the club
    Whispering to Mrs. Frazer.
    The strumpet Helen's voice has changed,
    Altered by high fidelity and Faust.
    Ripeness, a bag of withered figs, is all
    Included in the dollar table d'hôte;
    Desire, a blindman's mark, the scum of thought,
    Is quoted falling on the Stock Exchange;
    The carrion crow of Cairo cries 'Conform!
    It's later than you think! Conform! Conform!' "

All wrong, all wrong—this jangle out of tune
And out of context, a compendium
Of mixed quotations, a small orchestra
Of strident brass and clashing symbols.
Grimly he ventured on a final trial,
A third and last resort, an ultimate style. . . .

He found the very place, a School of Schools,
In a Midwestern grove of academe,
Half library, half laboratory, where
Strange cultures flourished in the filtered air.
"Poetry should not mean but be," cried one.
Whereat another scornfully replied,
"A poem lives by infinite meanings; it

Is all things to all readers, a complex
Of ambiguities that glide along
A dozen levels simultaneously.
The text is less important than the texture!"

He sighed and, desperately, tried once more.

    "The false dawn of appearance drowns
    The old, recurrent dream of long delay;
    A chaos of improvisation crowns
    The arrogant, ignoble day
        That crawls away.

    "Here, where the incidence of love bisects
    The arc of history, is heaped her hair.
    And, schooled by all the warring analects,
    I learn a style, a *savoir-faire*
        From a despair."

This was the last! He threw away his notes,
Facing the fact that he no longer was
In fashion. He had lost his following,
Lost her, lost everything except the pain,
The hard compulsion to create. . . .
                    There lay
The still unbroken lute. He took it up,
Tightened the strings, and knew that he must sing
For no reward, no audience, no response,
Only for that last listener, himself.

There was a rustling, then a gentle roar.
A lion arched against him. Singing birds
Cascaded on his shoulders. A fierce wolf
Offered a trusting paw, curled at his feet.
The forests clapped their hands, the trees bowed down.
And, more than all the miracles, she rose
With reassurance and without surprise,
Meeting his look with rediscovering eyes.

5

Here in these hills the Spring comes slow
  To those who learn her backwood way,
Who plough in ice and reap in snow.

First, there's a tremor; then, a throe;
  Then splintering of bells that play
"Hear!" In these hills the Spring comes slow.

We are not tricked for long. We know
  The paradox of frost in May,
Who plough in ice and reap in snow.

A mole sniffs the new earth; a crow
  Measures our field, decides to stay.
(Here in these hills the Spring comes slow.)

These are our vernal auguries. We go,
  Stopping at times to curse or pray,
Who plough in ice and reap in snow.

Suddenly white is green, although
  When it occurred we cannot say,
Who plough in ice and reap in snow,
Here in these hills . . .
             The Spring comes slow.

As Earth Was

When the last door is opened and flesh-free the loosed feet hasten
  Strange but unstumbling down a light-pathed meadow of air,
I shall find you once more and know you, not only by ewer and
    basin,
  But they will be there.

Around you a breath like a tune or a luminous fragrance will
    waver;
  And by this, this alone, I will know that truth has come true.
You will not be translated nor changed; the salt of your words,
    the savor
  Of your hands will be you.

For a while I shall sleep, travel-tired, and only your wake-note
    shall rouse me;
  And I shall take comfort in comfort, nor question nor think.
Once more your excess will be lavish to heal me and house me,
  My food and my drink.

The fiery circle will bind and the loving goad will be driven
  Nor feebler nor stronger than now, compliant no less to their
    laws.
And earth at its peak will be lifted to heaven, and heaven
  Will be as earth was.

A Side Street

I see them always there,
Upon the low, smooth wall before the church;
That row of little girls who sit and stare
Like sparrows on a granite perch.
They come in twittering couples or walk alone
To their gray bough of stone,
Sometimes by twos and threes, sometimes as many as five—
But always they sit there on the narrow coping
Bright-eyed and solemn, scarcely hoping
To see more than what is merely moving and alive.
They hear the couples pass; the lisp of happy feet
Increases and the night grows suddenly sweet.

Before the quiet church that smells of death
They sit.
And Life sweeps past them with a rushing breath,
And reaches out and plucks them by the hand,
And calls them boldly, whispering to each
In some strange speech
They tremble to but cannot understand.
It thrills and troubles them, as one by one,
The days run off like water through a sieve;
While, with a gaze as candid as the sun,
Poignant and puzzled and inquisitive,
They come and sit,
A part of life and yet apart from it.

At the Bottom of the Well

Something befell
   Young Adam Hope,
Who had a well
   For a telescope

In which the stars
   Came crystal-clear,
Brighter than Mars
   Or Jupiter,

Till Adam scarcely
   Looked at the sky,
Strewn so sparsely,
   Stretched so high.

Night after night,
   The neighbors tell,
He put out the light,
   He stole to the well.

To that dark funnel
   He came to pray,
"If only the sun'll
   Stay away,

"And nothing occurs
   Until I finish,
One of those stars
   Will forget to vanish,

"And when that late one
   Loafs and lingers,
I'll catch a great one
   With my fingers."

Adam's aim
  Grew fixed and stronger.
Then one night came
  That lasted longer

Than nights should last
  By natural law;
And when it passed
  The neighbors saw

Something that glistened
  Deep in the well.
They looked; they listened;
  They could not tell

The tale's conclusion.
  At the end of the rope
Was it truth, or illusion,
  Or Adam Hope?

A Wry Rondeau

Cum tu, Lydia, Telephi
cervicem roseam, cerea Telephi . . .
—HORACE, ODE 13, BOOK I

Cum tu, Lydia . . . you know the rest.
Praising the waxen arms and breast
 Of Telephus you drove me mad;
 You made the sunniest moments sad,
While tortures racked my heaving chest.

O, I could see you lightly dressed,
Inciting him with amorous zest,
 And hear you whisper low, "Dear lad,
   Come to Lydia."

Would it were over. I protest
Bruised lips and shoulders roughly pressed.
 O, gain your senses, leave the cad,
 And turn and listen as I add:
"Awake! Love is no giddy jest!
   Come to! Lydia!"

Beginning Again

Blackness that had no bounds at all
    Comes to an edge.
The ghost of a wind begins to crawl
    Over the ridge,
Blowing, with neither body nor light,
    Something in
That takes possession and makes the night
    Small and thin.
Too deep for sound, a vibration starts;
    Like a breath held back,
Darkness shrinks to its borders, parts,
    And into each crack
A trickle of lilac, a runnel of rose
    Widens the least
River of light as the air overflows,
    Defining the East.
One star persists; is snuffed out by
    A finger of blue.
A blackbird puts five clean holes in the sky,
    And day pours through.

Bird as Prophet

This is the day of a bird:

A hoping, hesitant third,
Groping for words with an eye
On the open volume of sky.
Then, though his call is to sing,
All of him turns to wing;
Banking his body where
On a long smooth flank of air
He learns to float—
Halfway between a miracle and a mote.

At last his throat!
He thinks of a fountain; and note
Follows note like links in a chain
Of white summer rain.
Spray after spray is upthrown:
Little hosannahs of tone,
Prophetic yet, somehow, profane.
Thus air and errand are done
(He and his prayer being one)
Whether he's heard or unheard.

This is the way of a bird.

Boy and Tadpoles

He brought them from the muddy creek
   And clapped them in this glassy sphere;
He studies them but does not speak
   While they flash by and disappear.
They curve and veer, they swerve and roll,
   A world of brown and yellow gleams—
Six tadpoles in a green glass bowl.
   He watches them—and dreams:

Slack water and a burnished moon.
What ship is that in the black lagoon?
Over an oily sea she slips
And drips a phosphorescent spray.
One hears the rattle of dice at play,
The cheers and clatter of drunken quips,
And thick lips roaring a ribald tune.
Her sides are gashed and pitted and scarred
And marred with slashes of brilliant rust.
Is it blood that glows like an evil crust?
Or mud that has grown like a stone, fixed hard
On this ill-starred vessel of loot and lust?

What's that? That spot on the faint horizon?
They glue their eyes on the tossing dot.
It crosses the moon like a curious blot,
While furious cries of "Blast 'em!" and "Pizen!"
Reveal that the missing prize has been sought for
And soon will be caught, for the little speck,
Towering in size, turns round the neck
Of forbidden land with its hidden ship;
Pauses, inquires, and fires a shot.
Crash! There's the clash of cutlass and sword.
Gun-barrels flash on the swarming deck.
The storming-party surges aboard.
A hot wind scourges; bullets whip

The figures that stumble in blood that is poured
In a tumbling flood through the crumbling night,
And stains the white dawn with a hideous light.

Ripples of dappled crimson and brown
Show where the sloops have grappled and split.
Here's where *The Royal Ben* went down;
And there, ten yards to the right of it,
The Black Avenger, full to the guards,
Riding the track of a lone disgrace,
Sank in her own dank hiding-place.
Nothing's afloat but the broken shards,
A boat and an oaken beam or two.
What of the captain? What of the crew?
Go, ask the sharks in the dark and bloody
Depths where the clean green tides turn muddy.
Ask of those bloated bellies that veer
In the ruddy welter that shelters them all.
Ask, as they plash their watery wall,
Before they flash and disappear,
And dwindle . . . and shrink . . . and sink to their hole . . .
And change . . . to . . . little things . . . with gleams,
Describing rings as they curve . . . and roll. . . .
Six tadpoles in a green glass bowl—
He watches them and dreams:

A sea of lapis lazuli,
With casual sunbeams lacing gold
On light skiffs facing the west, on old
Bright cliffs that rise from some mythical story,
On clouds that rest on the promontory,
On waves that reach white arms to the beach.
Sparkle and shimmer . . . glimmer and shine.
The sea grows dimmer, and darkens . . . like wine.
Who is that swimmer, untiring, returning,
Churning the brine?
Is it Leander, that daring boy?

Those skiffs? Agamemnon's? That cliff? Is it Troy?
A glow of sea-faring, home-yearning faces
Flares like a torch through these burning spaces.
The sea is turning a livelier hue.
Pools of the sun are gold oases
On a sweeping plain of purple and blue.
And—leap and curve—and swerve and flicker—
And—dip and swirl—with a flip of the tail,
The dolphins, coming faster, thicker,
Dive through the alabaster foam.
Under a sapphire dome they sail
And scale the breakers that drive them home.

But what is advancing in radiant vesture?
A mock sun dancing, it floats along.
Notes of a song, low, gradient cries
Rise from the image—or is it a god
Come to revisit the haunts of his youth.
Fable or truth—can the boy trust his eyes?
There, with bright hair, like a tossing fire,
Crossing the sunset, a Shape with a lyre
Calls to the tides . . . where no being has trod!
He guides his strange courser with never a rein;
And spurring the jeweled sides of a slender
Dolphin that glides on this rollicking lane,
Apollo rides in his antique splendor.

And, during it all, the dolphins are leaping,
Sweeping their silver-tipped tails in a sway
Of rhythms so gay that they play without sleeping;
Dancing and dipping, glancing and flipping
Sparks from the arcs they describe in the spray.
Mirth that is bounded by nothing but clear
Earth, sea and sky in a high, hollow sphere.
Spirit-surrounded, with tingling elation,
The green shuttles fly and a subtle persuasion,
A magic, half-Asian, invites him away.

16

A mingling of patterns and echoes and themes
Swim through his fancy like runaway streams.
A dim, shifting blur of disaster and drifting,
Of blood flowing faster, of livelier measures,
Of treasures, and time, and secret veils lifting . . .
And heroes . . . and tadpoles . . . and dreams.

109

Boy's First Night in the Tropics

Was that the forest coming or the wind?
And why should they be threatening little boys?
He could not see the moon, but knew it grinned
Behind the jalousies. There was a noise
Of chuckling evil, nameless scraping things,
The giving way of earth, the rise of stones,
Grasses that moved with horrid whisperings,
And dead palmettos rubbing their dry bones.

Sleep came and went like a high wind; it blew
His dreams down from their last heroic height.
He knew the jaws, the snapped sword, now; he knew
More than a hero's heart should know of fright.
Lost, in the crouching dark, he listened to
The thickly breathing, dragon-haunted night.

Burning Bush

And suddenly the flowing night stands still
    And the loose air grows tense and small;
Runners of flame from nowhere rise and fill
    The narrowest veins, till all

The martyrdom of fire is not enough
    For bodies eager to be doomed;
Burning in one long agony of love,
    Burning but not consumed.

And the last blaze leaps from our being's core
    And flesh, too shaken to rejoice,
Cries out till quiet, vaster than before,
    Speaks in the still, small voice.

Caliban in the Coal Mines

God, we don't like to complain.
   We know that the mine is no lark.
But—there's the pools from the rain;
   But—there's the cold and the dark.

God, You don't know what it is—
   You, in Your well-lighted sky,
Watching the meteors whizz;
   Warm, with a sun always by.

God, if You had but the moon
   Stuck in Your cap for a lamp,
Even You'd tire of it soon,
   Down in the dark and the damp.

Nothing but blackness above,
   And nothing that moves but the cars. . . .
God, if You wish for our love,
   Fling us a handful of stars!

Coal Fire

And once, in some swamp forest, these,
My child, were trees.
Before there was a thing to run,
These dead black chips were one
Green net to hold the sun.
Each leaf in turn was taught the right
Way to drink light.
The smallest twigs were made to learn
How to catch flame and yet not burn.
Branch and then bough began to eat
Their diet of heat.
And so for years, ten million years, or higher,
They held that fire.

And now, from these old splinters that remain,
The fire is loose again.
See how its hundred hands reach here and there,
Fingering the air.
Then, growing bolder, twisting free,
It fastens on the remnants of the tree
And, one by one, consumes them, mounts beyond them, leaps, is
      done,
And goes back to the sun.

Country Evening

This is the time when birds no longer cry
    Haphazardly and high,
Nor dot the rails nor punctuate the trees
    In swift apostrophes.
This is the time day hesitates, as though
    It almost feared to go,
And the great span that promised to remain
    Goes back into thin rain.
And, doubtful of itself, night throws one spark
    To blaze the trail of dark;
And earth gives off cool breaths, green-growing smells,
    And something else
That lingers between light and atmosphere;
    And the third star swings clear.
This is the hour for lamps; this is the time
    For the slow, homeward climb.

Critique of Pure Rhyme

Finished and flawless,
　Crisply designed,
Here is the aweless
　Breath of the mind.
Light without glamor
　Illumines this world;
Chisel and hammer
　Shape all these curled
Odorless petals,
　Keen, cutting fronds,
Into bright metals
　Harder than bronze.
Thin as old glass
　Still undemolished,
Even the grass
　Is painted and polished,
Spun out and waved,
　Carefully counted,
Lacquered, engraved,
　And finally mounted
With so many millions
　Of jewels for color
That even the brilliance
　Grows duller and duller.
Rhyme, like a shutter,
　Claps through the words.
Mechanical birds
　Woodenly flutter.
Clouds of pale cardboard
　Creak through the sky;
While with a hard, bored,
　Baffled eye,
We turn from these mobile
　Toys that are offered,
Seeking a noble

Phrase that has suffered.
But in this airless
   Vacuum
Nothing so careless
   Can ever come.
Never a burden,
   A cry or a curse
Can hope to be heard in
   This crackling verse.
Its one endeavor
   Is to be smooth;
Hard and clever,
   Its highest truth.
Without a blunder,
   It stiffens and dies—
What might have been wonder
   Is scarcely surprise.

Design for a Perfect World

I said the sun had never burned for you;
That yours was still a world of glacial light
And frozen ecstasy. An icy blue
Hardened your heavens, while a bright
Moon-lacquered glitter that could never glow
Flashed on an iron earth: a sharp, unreal
Dominion that you forced yourself to feel
And no warm child of earth could live to know.

But now I learned that such things could be so.
A freezing wind had blown through last night's rain
And sealed the flowing earth into a plain
Of rigid fantasy. A heaven of ice
Flattened the rocks that turned against the skies
Their mirrors of cold steel. The stiffened grass
Thrust wire-like blades in scabbards of thin glass.
Here were hard gems and harder jewelleries
Set in rock-crystal. Here the metal trees
Were all bronze trunks, gold twigs and copper boughs,
With every burnished leaf hammered and curled,
Like wooden branches on the prows
Of battered ships. No wind that blew could rouse
This tinsel and metallic world.

Here was your carved and final purity
That shone and kept its brilliance without heat;
A clean and passionless retreat,
Purged of disquiet, fear, imperfect song.
And you were right, it seems, and I was wrong.
Here's peace at last, cooler than ivory,
Flawlessly shaped, a world in filigree.
And you can live in it. But not with me.

Disenchantment

Here is the German
   Fairy forest;
And here I turn in,
   I, the poorest
Son of an aging
   Humble widow.
The light is fading;
   Every shadow
Conceals a kobold,
   A gnome's dark eye,
Or even some troubled
   Lorelei.
A ruined castle
   Invites me to prowl;
Its only vassal
   A frightened owl
(Most likely a princess
   Under a spell)—
And what light dances
   Behind that well?
Perhaps great riches
   Are hidden there,
Perhaps a witch's
   Magic snare.
I walk up boldly,
   Though my breath falters;
But no one holds me,
   Nothing alters
Except the dying
   Phosphorescence,
Where the rocks lie in
   Broken crescents.
These rocks are haunted,
   Everyone says,
And here the enchanted

Dragon obeys
Only the youngest
Son of a widow,
Who waits the longest,
Fearing no shadow
Of any uncommon
Phantom in metal,
But dares to summon
The Thing to battle.
I've said my vespers,
I've tightened my gloves;
The forest whispers
And chuckles and moves.
Darker and closer
The stillness surges.
Not even the ghost of
A rabbit emerges.
I rattle my weapons,
I call and I call
But nothing happens,
Nothing at all.

Nothing at all.

Doomsday at Weggis

When Gabriel came to Weggis that last morning
They thought it was the postman with the papers,
And no one noticed him and his forewarning
Except old Franz, who, friendlier than the neighbors,
Hailed him with *"Grüss Gott"* and resumed his plowing.
The rest were far too occupied with haying
Or pulling beets or scrubbing floors or sewing
To stop and hear what Gabriel was saying.
"Prepare!" he called, the urgency grown greater,
"Doomsday! Doomsday! Doomsday!" But no one heeded;
They had no time for trivial things till later.
No one. He cupped his hands. He railed. He pleaded.
He roared until his holy features reddened,
Shouting to rouse the dead. . . .
                    Then he succeeded.
The dogs of Switzerland, like one dog maddened,
Flew at his heels and snapped, till Gabriel straightway
(His errand done, his message given) departed
In uncelestial haste behind the gateway.

By now ten thousand echoing throats were started,
And out of moldy barns and bones unburied
Came ghastly howls and yammerings and bellows;
And not one voice but broke its leash and hurried
To spread the violent rumor to its fellows,
Who, knowing tales more terrible, grew jealous
And answered back and bayed and whined and worried,
Barking the ghost of Gabriel up the hill.

Since then no dog in Weggis has been still.

Elegy

These hands, two nimble butterflies,
   I never saw them at rest;
Nor knew a tide so regular
   Could move through your stormy breast.
You loved to meet life dancing
   With glistening steps, till all
Your fluent body seemed a curve
   In a restless waterfall.

And now you lie here so coldly,
   So unbelievably still;
A stone on a marble river,
   Ice on a wintry hill.
Something has made your beauty
   Inscrutable and grave;
Holding your once warm body
   In the curve of a frozen wave.

Envy

The willow and the river
  Ripple with silver speech,
And one refrain forever
  They murmur each to each:

"Brook with the silver gravel,
  Would that your lot were mine;
To wander free, to travel
  Where greener valleys shine.
Strange ventures, fresh revealings,
  And, at the end, the sea.
Brook, with your turns and wheelings,
  How rich your life must be."

"Tree with the golden rustling,
  Would that I were so blessed,
To cease this stumbling, jostling,
  This feverish unrest.
I join the ocean's riot;
  You stand song-filled and free.
Tree, with your peace and quiet,
  How rich your life must be."

The willow and the river
  Ripple with silver speech,
And one refrain forever
  They murmur each to each.

Equals

You child, how can you dare complain
    That you and I may be mismated
Because, you say, you lack a brain
    And I'm so highly educated.

The body is the greater thing;
    And you are greatly gifted when
You have such hands and breasts that bring
    More peace than all the words of men.

Take pride in this, your beauty; drink
    The wine it offers for our love.
Be glad you do not have to think.
    One thoughtful lover is enough!

We're equal partners, that is plain;
    Our life cannot grow dull or shoddy,
While I have such a lovely brain
    And you have such a lively body.

Eve Speaks

Pause, God, and ponder, ere Thou judgest me.
Though it be Doomsday, and the trampling winds
Rush blindly through the stark and cowering skies,
Bearing Thy fearful mandate like a sword,
I do not tremble. I am unafraid.
Though the red flame of wrath lick up the worlds,
And dizzy stars fall in a golden rain;
Though, in an agonizing fear of life,
The summoned spirits, torn from gentle graves,
Whirl at Thy feet or fly before Thy frown,
Like leaves that run before a scornful breeze,
I do not fly. My soul is unafraid.
Years have swept over me and in the wash
Of foaming centuries have been forgot;
Yet still my soul remembers Paradise,
That perfect echo of Thy gentler mood.
Wrapped in a drowsy luxury we lived,
Beauty our food and idleness our pillow.
Day after day, we walked beneath Thy smile;
And, as we wandered through the glittering hours,
Our souls unfolding with the friendly earth,
Eden grew richer to our ardent eyes.
With every step, a clump of trees, a star,
An undiscovered flower, a hill, a cry,
A new, wild sunset or a wilder bird
Entered our lives and grew a part of us.
Lord, there was naught but happiness—and yet,
Though Adam gloried in the world's content,
And sunned himself in rich complacency,
The thought that there was something more than joy,
Beyond perfection, greater than singing peace
And tranquil happiness, vexed all my hours.
Here in a garden, without taint or care,
We played like children, we who were not children.
Swaddled with ease, lulled with Thy softest dreams,

We lived in perfect calm, who were not perfect.
Eden was made for angels, not for Man.

Often the thought of this would come to me
When Adam's songs seemed empty of all mirth,
When he grew moody, and the reckless fire
Leaped in his eyes and died; or when I saw
Him lying at my side—his brawny arms
Knotted with strength; his bosom deep and broad;
His hands tight-clenched, his mouth firm, even in sleep.
Here was a body made for mighty building,
Here was a brain designed to dream and mould—
To waste such energy on such a life!
I could not think it. Seeing him, I knew
Man made for Eden only, not for more,
Was made in vain. I claimed my Adam, God;
Claimed him for fiercer things and lustier worlds,
Immoderate measures, insolent desires;
Claimed him for great and strengthening defeats.
He was but one of many things to Thee—
A cunning lump of clay, a speaking clod—
One of a universe of miracles.
Each day a fresh creation was to Thee;
Thou hadst infinity to shape and guard—
I only Adam.

Lying awake one night beneath the Tree,
I heard him sighing in a fitful sleep.
A cold, disdainful moon mocked my unrest;
A night-bird circled out beyond the wood.
Never did Eden seem so much a prison.
Past the great gates I glimpsed the unknown world,
Lying unfettered in majestic night.
I saw the broadening stream hold out its arms;
The proud hills called me, and the teasing lure
Of things unheard, unguessed at caught my soul.
Adam was made for this—and this for him.
The peace of Eden grew intolerable.

Better the long uncertainty of toil,
The granite scorn of the experienced world,
And failure upon failure; better these
Than this enforced and rotting indolence.
Adam should know his godhood; he should feel
The weariness of work, and pride of it;
The agony of creation, and its reward.
His hands should rear the dream, his sinews think;
And in a rush of power his strength should rise
And rend, and tame, and wrest its secret from
The sweating, energetic earth,
Until his rude and stumbling soul could grasp
Conquering and unconquerable joys.
So should his purpose work among the stars;
Face, without fear, contemptuous centuries;
Meet the astonished heavens with a laugh,
And answer God with God's own words and deeds.
One thing alone would give all this to him,
One thing would cleave the sealed and stubborn rocks,
Harness the winds, yoke the unbridled seas:
Knowledge, the force and shaper of the world.

And so I knew that we should eat, and learn.

Pause, God, and ponder, ere Thou judgest me.

Fairmount Cemetery

Of all the nooks discovered,
  I like our first love best;
That screened-off bit of hillside,
  A soft, green nest.

A stream uncoiled beyond us;
  Trees shook their smoky plumes;
And, like a still procession,
  Marched the white tombs.

How often we would come there
  To love and talk of love;
The cemetery below us,
  All heaven above.

And do you still remember
  The solemn pledge we tried
To write in blood and could not?
  And how you cried?

And how I dared the future
  With many a pompous speech?
"What," I stormed, "can touch us
  Whom death cannot reach!

"Pain shall discard his dagger;
  Care shall avert his face;
Defeated years shall triumph
  In our embrace!

"Rapt as two young conquerors,
  We shall laugh and know
Life is all that matters.
  We have made it so.

"Life is all that matters;
   Love is all that saves" . . .
Then I heard the dead men
   Chuckling in their graves.

Fantastic Bird

A bird ran up the onyx steps of night,
   Seeking the moon upon her silver throne;
But stars confused him with their insolent light
   And left him in the friendless skies, alone.

He watched the winds, disheveled and awry,
   Hurling the clouds, like pillows, from their beds;
He saw the mountain-peaks that nudged the sky
   Take off the wreaths of sunset from their heads.

He heard the storms, a troupe of headstrong boys,
   Locked up as punishment for petulant tears,
Beat on the ebony doors with such a noise
   That all the angels had to hold their ears.

Frightened, he left the halls of thundering sound
   For a less dazzling height, a lowlier dream;
And, perching on a watery bough, he found
   The moon, her white laugh rippling from the stream.

Folk-Song

Back she came through the trembling dusk;
   And her mother spoke and said:
"What is it makes you late today,
And why do you smile and sing as gay
   As though you just were wed?"
"Oh, mother, my hen that never had chicks
   Has hatched out six!"

Back she came through the flaming dusk;
   And her mother spoke and said:
"What gives your eyes that dancing light,
What makes your lips so strangely bright,
   And why are your cheeks so red?"
"Oh, mother, the berries I ate in the lane
   Have left a stain."

Back she came through the faltering dusk;
   And her mother spoke and said:
"You are weeping; your footstep is heavy with care—
What makes you totter and cling to the stair,
   And why do you hang your head?"
"Oh, mother—oh, mother—you never can know.
   I loved him so!"

Food and Drink

Why has our poetry eschewed
The rapture and response of food?
What hymns are sung, what prayers are said
For home-made miracles of bread?
Since what we love has always found
Expression in enduring sound,
Music and verse should be competing
To match the transient joy of eating.
There should be present in our songs
As many tastes as there are tongues;
There should be humbly celebrated
One passion that is never sated.

Let us begin it with the first
Distinction of a conscious thirst
When the collusion of the vine
Uplifted water into wine.
Let us give thanks before we turn
To other things of less concern
For all the poetry of the table:
Clams that parade their silent fable;
Lobsters that have a rock for stable;
Red-faced tomatoes ample as
A countryman's full-bosomed lass;
Plain-spoken turnips; honest beets;
The carnal gusto of red meats;
The wood-fire pungence of smoked ham;
The insipidity of lamb;
Young veal that's smooth as natural silk;
The lavish motherliness of milk;
Parsley and lemon-butter that add
Spring sweetness unto river shad;
Thin flakes of halibut and cod,
Pickerel, flounder, snapper, scrod,
And every fish whose veins may be

Charged with the secrets of the sea;
Sweet-sour carp, beloved by Jews;
Pot-luck simplicity of stews;
Crabs, juiciest of Nature's jokes;
The deep reserve of artichokes;
Mushrooms, whose taste is texture, loath
To tell of their mysterious growth;
Quick, mealy comfort glowing in
A baked potato's crackled skin;
The morning promise, hailed by man,
Of bacon crisping in the pan;
The sage compound of *Hasenpfeffer*
With dumplings born of flour and zephyr;
Corn that is roasted in the ash;
The eternal compromise of hash;
Spinach whose spirit is the soil;
Anchovies glorified in oil;
The slow-gold nectar maples yield;
Pale honey tasting of the field
Where every clover is Hymettus;
The cooling sanity of lettuce,
And every other herbal green
Whose touch is calm, whose heart is clean;
Assertive leek; rank chard; the boast
Of *nouveaux riches:* a quail on toast;
Succulent bean-sprouts; bamboo-shoots;
The sapid catalogue of fruits:
Plebeian apple; caustic grape;
Quinces that have no gift for shape;
Dull plums that mind their own affairs;
Incurably bland and blunted pears;
Fantastic passion-fruit; frank lemons
With acid tongues as sharp as women's;
Exotic loquats; sly persimmons;
White currants; amber-fleshed sultanas
(Miniature and sweetened mannas);
Expansive peaches; suave bananas;
Oranges ripening in crates;

Tight-bodied figs; sun-wrinkled dates;
Melons that have their own vagaries;
The bright astringency of berries;
Curds that are strained through cotton sieves;
Snails that grow great on mulberry leaves;
Crêpe-satin luxury of cream;
Wedding-cake that fulfills the dream;
The esoteric lure of truffles;
The warm approach of well-timed waffles;
Pepper, whose satire stings and cuts;
The pointless persiflage of nuts;
Sauces of complex mysteries;
Proverbial parsnips; muscular cheese;
Innocent eggs that scorn disguises;
Languid molasses; burning spices
In kitchen-oracles to Isis;
Thick sauerkraut's fat-bellied savor;
Anything with a chocolate flavor;
Deep generosity of pies;
Rich puddings bursting to surprise;
The smug monotony of rice;
Raisins that doze in cinnamon buns;
Kentucky biscuits, Scottish scones;
Falstaffian tarts that mock the chaste
Rose-elegance of almond-paste;
Venison steaks that smack of cloisters;
Goose-liver for the soul that roisters;
Reticent prawn; Lucullan oysters;
Sausages, fragrant link on link. . . .

The vast ambrosias of drink:
Tea, that domestic mandarin;
Bucolic cider; loose-lipped gin;
Coffee, extract of common sense,
Purgative of the night's pretense;
Cocoa's prim nursery; the male
Companionship of crusty ale;
Cognac as oily as a ferret;

The faintly iron thrust of claret;
Episcopal port, aged and austere;
Rebellious must of grape; the clear,
Bluff confraternity of beer . . .

All these are good, all are a part
Of man's imperative needs that start
Not in the palate but the heart.
Thus fat and fiber, root and leaf
Become swift pleasure and slow grief.
These, through the chemistry of blood,
Sustain his hungering manhood,
Fulfilling passion, ripening pain;
Steel in his bone, fire at his brain.
So, until man abjures the meats
Terrestrial and impermanent sweets,
Growing beyond the things he eats,
Let us be thankful for the good
Beauty and benison of food;
Let us join chiming vowel with vowel
To rhapsodize fish, flesh, and fowl;
And let us thank God in our songs
There are as many tastes as tongues!

Never was landscape quite so clipped and callow
As this between these pale, bucolic covers:
On these smooth lawns the water-color lovers
Stray through the copse where kine and crocus follow;
And elms—elms lonely, leaning, haunted, hollow—
Are packed with thrushes, wrens, and wheeling plovers
As, over every sprig of thyme, there hovers
At least one curlew or nostalgic swallow.

Here, far beyond the reach of life or trams,
A world composed of ever-verdant vales
Is thick with darkling wings and thrice-told tales,
Blackbirds and buttercups and gentle dams;
While, from the hawthorn, immemorial lambs
Keep moonlit trysts with deathless nightingales.

Glad Day   (AFTER A COLOR PRINT BY BLAKE)

Come, day, glad day, day running out of the night
   With breast aflame and your generous arms outspread;
With hands that scatter the dawn and fingers busy with light,
   And a rainbow of fire to flicker about your head.

Come soon, glad day, come with the confident stride
   Of the sun in its march over mountains, of the wind on its way
      through the air;
Naked, and noble, and new, throwing the darkness aside;
   Come, with your gesture of space, and the heavens loosed in
      your hair.

For the waiting is lifeless, and dawn is a lingering doubt,
   And our feet are confused in shadows that tangle and rend.
Come, day, glad day, come with a wordless shout,
   Clean with rejoicing, complete in outgiving, come, day without
      end.

44

God's Youth

I often wish that I had been alive
Ere God grew old, before His eyes were tired
Of the eternal circlings of the sun,
Of the perpetual springs, the weary years
Forever marching on an unknown quest;
The yawning seasons pacing to and fro,
Like stolid sentinels to guard the earth.
I wish that I had been alive when He
Was still delighted with each casual thing
His mind could fashion, when His soul first thrilled
With childlike pleasure at the blooming sun,
When the first dawn met His enraptured eyes,
And the first prayers of men stirred in His heart.
With what a glow of pride He heard the stars
Rush by Him singing as they bravely leaped
Into the unexplored and endless skies,
Bearing His beauty, like a battle-cry.
Or watched the light, obedient to His will,
Spring out of nothingness to answer Him,
Hurling strange suns and planets in its joy
Of fiery freedom from the lifeless dark.
But more than all the splendid heavens He made,
The elements new-tamed, the harnessed worlds,
In spite of these, it must have pleased Him most
To feel Himself branch out, let go, dare all,
Give utterance to His vaguely formed desires,
And loose a flood of fancies, wild and frank.

Oh, those were noble times; those gay attempts,
Those vast and droll experiments that were made
When God was young and blithe and whimsical.
When, from the infinite humor of His heart,
He made the elk with such extravagant horns;
Monkeys, those leaping burlesques of themselves;
The loud, inane hyena; the grotesque

Incredible giraffe, whose silly head
Nibbles at stars lost in the leaves, his legs
Two pairs of monstrous clowns on circus stilts;
The paradox of the peacock, whose bright pomp
Is like a blazing trumpet, and whose voice
Is but the strident cackle of a joke;
The ostrich, like a snake tied to a bird,
All out of sense and drawing, wilder far
Than all the nightmare fancies formed by men;
The hump-backed camel, like a lump of clay,
Thumbed at for hours, and then thrown aside,
The elephant, with splendid, useless tooth,
And nose and arm and fingers all in one;
The hippopotamus, absurdly bland—
Oh, how God must have laughed when first He saw
These great jests breathe and love and walk about,
And how the heavens must have echoed Him!
For greater than His wisdom or His wrath
Was God's vast mirth before His back was bent
With time and all the troubling universe,
Ere He grew dull and weary with creating.

Oh, to have been alive and heard that laugh
Thrilling the stars, convulsing all the earth,
While meteors flashed from out His sparkling eyes,
And even the eternal, placid Night
Forgot to lift reproving fingers, smiled,
And joined indulgent in the merriment.
And how they sang, and how the hours flew
When God was young, and blithe, and whimsical.

Goliath and David

GOLIATH

See the dazzled stripling stand,
Naked as an empty hand.
And here am I, a clanking mass
Blotting out the yellow grass
With a body only sent
For the world's astonishment:
Arms as great as monstrous boughs
Where no bird would dare to house,
Fingers like some poisonous growth
Even jungle-beasts must loathe,
And a goggling head awry
Like a black moon in the sky.
Here I wait, uneagerly,
For the child that faces me,
Frightened by my length of limb—
And the clean, young grace of him
Unaware that cheek and brow
Taste their last of sunlight now.
Oh, that it were I, not he!
Oh, that God would take from me
This power only schooled in harm
And send it through that puny arm
With such a fire that it might well
Break through this hugely rotting shell.
But there will be no miracle.
There is no help. Young David, fly!
I am destruction's demon, aye,
Too sick to live, too strong to die.

DAVID

And there he looms, no more defiant
Than any hill. So that's a giant!
That is the thing that should alarm me
More than the sight of hell's own army

47

Commanded by its master devil.
But this—why, this is nothing evil.
Its eyes are cow's eyes; it looks civil;
A thing that only babes could fear.
Yet I—what am I doing here?
What part have I, the least of shepherds,
Among these hungry spears and scabbards?
What! Have I tended sheep and cattle
Only to lead the wolves to battle?
Am I possessed of howling demons
That I should seek the blood of humans?
God, take this madness out of me.
Give me my pastures, let me be—
Far from this clash of words and weapons—
Where nothing cries and little happens,
Save when a star leaps from the heavens
Or a new rush of song enlivens
The heart that beats in balanced measures,
Unshaken by more passionate seizures.
See, I will fling this silly pebble
Away from me to end my trouble
And pluck harp-strings again till they
Charm every darker thought away.
Come, old Goliath, come and play!

Grace without Meat TUSCAN STYLE

God of the grape whose veins are taught
  To make flesh of the sun,
Lord of the olive tree whose thought
  Brings oil out of the stone,

Father of fig and orange trees
  That laugh to bear their load,
Forgive us all our trespasses
  On thy too-tempting road.

And though thy children will be fed
  On what the Lord decrees,
Give us this day our daily bread—
  And wine and fruit and cheese.

Hairdressing

Before the prim old mirror
    That stands so stiffly there,
With puritan precision
    You rearrange your hair.

Knitting your childlike forehead,
    As, with a whimsical pout,
Your fingers, brisk and busy,
    Bring order out of rout.

But here a coil escapes you,
    And there a bright strand shakes
Over your neck and shoulder,
    In little yellow snakes.

Serious and ensnaring,
    Each skillful hand begins
To make an artful pattern
    Woven with puffs and pins.

You pause to turn and ask me
    How this appears, or that,
Till all is smoothed and finished
    With a last, careful pat.

My pretty, proper darling,
    With not one hair amiss,
Who turns, like some calm duty,
    One powdered cheek to kiss,

Are you the same wild creature
    I held last night, and found
Sleeping upon my shoulder
    With all her hair unbound?

Hands

Strange, how this smooth and supple joint can be
   Put to so many purposes. It checks
And rears the monsters of machinery,
   And shapes the idle gallantries of sex.

Those hands that light the fuse and dig the trap,
   Fingers that spin the earth or plunge through shame,
And yours, that lie so lightly in your lap,
   Are only blood and dust—all are the same.

What mastery directs them through the world
   And gives these delicate bones so great a power? . . .
You drop your head. You sleep. Your hands are curled
   Loosely, like some half-opened, perfumed flower.

An hour ago they burned in mine and sent
   Armies with banners charging through my veins.
Now they are cool and white; they rest content,
   Curved in a smile. The mystery remains.

Havens

Belovèd, let me grope and lie
   In the triumphant reaches of your soul;
That singing and barbaric sky
   Which is my goal.

Age cannot make the way less fresh;
   And bar me if I ever dare despise
The close and friendly house of flesh
   Through which it lies.

And slowly, slowly, let me move
   Toward every twist of passion, shrine or snare,
Through the dark labyrinth of love
   That leads me there.

He Goads Himself

And was it I that rose to rattle
  A broken lance against iron laws?
Was it I that asked to go down in battle
  For a lost cause?

Fool! Must there be new deaths to cry for
  When only rottenness survives!
Here are enough lost hopes to die for
  Through twenty lives.

What have we learned? That the familiar
  Lusts are the only things that endure;
That for a world grown blinder and sillier
  There is no cure.

And man? Free of one kind of fetter
  He runs to gaudier shackles and brands,
Deserving, for all of his groans, no better
  Than he demands.

The old routine of bed and barter,
  Birth and burial holds the lot.
Was it I that dreamed of being a martyr?
  How—and for what?

Yet, while the evil tides run stronger
  As life shrugs by without meaning or shape,
Let me know flame and the teeth of hunger;
  Storm, not escape.

Infidelity

You have not conquered me; it is the surge
    Of love itself that beats against my will;
It is the sting of conflict, the old urge
        That calls me still.

It is not you I love, it is the form
    And shadow of all lovers who have died
That gives you all the freshness of a warm
        And unfamiliar bride.

It is your name I breathe, your hands I seek;
    It will be you when you are gone;
And yet the dream, the name I cannot speak
        Is that which lures me on.

It is the golden summons, the bright wave
    Of banners calling me anew;
It is all passion, perilous and grave—
        It is not you.

Jerusalem Delivered

King David Hotel, Jerusalem, offers Tea Dances Wednesday and Saturday, Aperitif Concerts every Sunday, and Cocktail Parties in the Winter Garden.

—Adv. in the *Palestine News*

Miriam, strike your cymbal,
 Young David, add your voice;
Once more the tribes are nimble,
 Once more the Jews rejoice.

Beneath the flowering mango
 Where peace and perfume drip,
Solomon does the tango
 And Sheba shakes a hip.

Rebekah trots with Aaron,
 Deborah treads the earth,
Fresh as the Rose of Sharon
 With evening gowns by Worth.

Susannah meets the Elders
 With an increased regard;
Pounds, dollars, marks, and guilders
 Receive their due award.

Jerusalem the Golden,
 With milk and honey blest,
Revive the rapt and olden
 Ardor within each breast;

Add Gilead to Gomorrah;
 Fling torches through the dark;
Dancing before the Torah,
 With cocktails at the Ark!

Jewish Lullaby

Husha, O husha,
　And lull-lullaby;
No mother in Russia
　Is prouder than I.
You stumble no longer,
　Soon you will run,
And you will grow stronger
　Than Samson, my son.

You will be famous,
　Your thoughts will go wide;
Isaiah and Amos
　Will walk at your side.
Your words will be graven
　On metal and stone;
And the Great Ones in Heaven
　Will envy my son.

Last Words before Winter

All my sheep
Gather in a heap,
For I spy the woolly, woolly wolf.

Farewell, my flocks,
Farewell. But let me find you
Safe in your stall and barn and box
With your winter's tale behind you.

Farewell, my cattle (both).
I leave you just as loath
As though you were a hundred head,
Instead
Of two-and-a-half.
(Two cows and a calf.)

Farewell, my apple trees;
You have learned what it is to freeze,
With the drift on your knees.
But, oh, beware
Those first kind days, the snare
Of the too promising air
The cost
Of over-sudden trust—
And then the killing frost.

Farewell, belovèd acres;
I leave you in the hands
Of one whose earliest enterprise was lands:
Your Maker's.

Yard, hutch, and house, farewell.
It is for you to tell
How you withstood the great white wolf, whose fell

Is softer than a lambkin's, but whose breath
Is death.

Farewell, hoof, claw, and wing,
Finned, furred, and feathered thing,
Till Spring—

All my sheep
Gather in a heap,
For I spy the woolly, woolly wolf.

Long Feud

Where, without bloodshed, can there be
A more relentless enmity
Than the long feud fought silently

Between man and the growing grass.
Man's the aggressor, for he has
Weapons to humble and harass

The impudent spears that charge upon
His sacred privacy of lawn.
He mows them down, and they are gone

Only to lie in wait, although
He builds above and digs below
Where never a root would dare to go.

His are the triumphs till the day
There's no more grass to cut away;
And, weary of labor, weary of play,

Having exhausted every whim,
He stretches out each conquering limb.
And then the small grass covers him.

Matter

When I was a live man
   A few years ago,
For all I might say,
   For all I could do

I got no attention;
   My life was so small
The world didn't know
   I was living at all.

Such stolid indifference
   I couldn't allow;
I swore that I'd matter—
   Never mind how.

But after a lifetime
   Of hunger and prayer,
I broke my heart trying
   To make the world care.

And now as I lie here,
   Feeding this tree,
I am more to the world
   Than it is to me.

Monolog from a Mattress

Heinrich Heine, 56, speaks:

Can that be you, *la mouche?* Wait till I lift
This palsied eyelid and make sure. . . . Ah, true.
Come in, dear fly, and pardon my delay
In thus existing; I can promise you
Next time you come you'll find no dying poet.
Without sufficient spleen to see me through,
The joke becomes too tedious a jest.
I am afraid my mind is dull today;
I have that—something—heavier on my chest,
And then, you see, I've been exchanging thoughts
With Doctor Franz. He talked of Kant and Hegel
As though he'd nursed them both through whooping cough,
And, as he left, he let his finger shake
Too playfully, as though to say, "Now off
With that long face—you've years and years to live."
I think he thinks so. But, for Heaven's sake,
Don't credit it—and never tell Mathilde.
Poor dear, she has enough to bear already.

This *was* a month! During my lonely weeks
One person actually climbed the stairs
To seek a cripple. It was Berlioz—
But Berlioz always was original!
Meissner was also here; he caught me unawares,
Scribbling to my old mother. "What!" he cried,
"Is the old lady of the *Dammthor* still alive?
And do you write her still?" "Each month or so."
"And is she not unhappy then, to find
How wretched you must be?" "How can she know?
You see," I laughed, "she thinks I am as well
As when she saw me last. She is too blind
To read the papers—someone else must tell
What's in my letters, merely signed by me.
Thus she is happy. For my other woes—

63

That any son should be as sick as I,
No mother could believe."

                                   Ja, so it goes.

Come here, my lotus-flower. It is best
I drop the mask today; the half-cracked shield
Of mockery calls for younger hands to wield.
Laugh—or I'll hug it closer to my breast.
So . . . I can be as mawkish as I choose
And give my thoughts an airing, let them loose
For one last rambling stroll before— Now look!
Why tears? You never heard me say "the end."
Before . . . before I clap them in a book
And so get rid of them once and for all.
This is their holiday—we'll let them run—
Some have escaped already. There goes one.
What, I have often mused, did Goethe mean?
So many years ago at Weimar, Goethe said,
"Heine has all the poet's gifts but love."
Good God! But that is all I ever had.
More than enough! So much of love to give
That no one gave me any in return.
And so I flashed and snapped in my own fires
Until I stood, with nothing left to burn,
A twisted trunk, in chilly isolation.
Ein Fichtenbaum steht einsam—you recall?
I was that Northern tree and, in the South,
Amalia. . . . So I turned to scornful cries,
Hot iron songs to save the rest of me;
Plunging the brand in my own misery.
Crouching behind my pointed wall of words,
Ramparts I built of moons and loreleis,
Enchanted roses, sphinxes, love-sick birds,
Giants, dead lads who left their graves to dance,
Fairies, and phoenixes, and friendly gods—
A curious frieze, half Renaissance, half Greek,
Behind which, in revulsion of romance,
I lay and laughed—and wept—till I was weak.

Words were my shelter, words my one escape.
Words were my weapons against everything.
Was I not once the son of Revolution?
Give my the lyre, I said, and let me sing
My song of battle: Words like furious stars,
Shot down with power to burn the palaces;
Words like bright javelins to fly with fierce
Hate of the oily Philistines and glide
Through all the seven heavens till they pierce
The pious hypocrites who dare to creep
Into the Holy Places. "Then," I cried,
"I am a fire to rend and roar and leap;
I am all joy and song, all sword and flame!"
Ha—you observe me passionate. I aim
To curb these wild emotions lest they soar
Or drive against my will. (So I have said
These many years—and still they are not tame.)
Scraps of a song keep rumbling in my head.
Listen—you never heard me sing before.

> When a false world betrays your trust
>   And stamps upon your fire,
> When what seemed blood is only rust,
>   Take up the lyre.

> How quickly the heroic mood
>   Responds to its own ringing;
> The scornful heart, the doubtful blood
>   Leap upward, singing!

Ah, that was how it used to be. But now,
Du schöner Todesengel, it is odd
How more than calm I am. Franz said it shows
Power of religion, and it does, perhaps—
Religion, or morphine, or poultices—God knows.
I sometimes have a sentimental lapse
And long for saviours and a physical God.
When health is all used up, when money goes,

When courage cracks and leaves a shattered will,
Then Christianity begins. For a sick Jew,
It is a very good religion. . . . Still,
I fear that I will die as I have lived,
A long-nosed heathen playing with his scars,
A pagan killed by *Weltschmerz*. . . . I remember,
Once when I stood with Hegel at a window,
I, being full of bubbling youth and coffee,
Spoke in symbolic tropes about the stars.
Something I said about "those high
Abodes of all the blest" provoked his temper.
"Abodes? The stars?" He froze me with a sneer,
"A light eruption on the firmament."
"But," cried romantic I, "is there no sphere
Where virtue is rewarded when we die?"
And Hegel mocked, "A very pleasant whim.
So you demand a bonus since you spent
One lifetime and refrained from poisoning
Your testy grandmother!" . . . How much of him
Remains in me, even when I am caught
In dreams of death and immortality.

To be eternal—what a brilliant thought!
It must have been conceived and coddled first
By some old shopkeeper in Nuremberg,
His slippers warm, his children amply nursed,
Who, with his lighted meerschaum in his hand,
His nightcap on his head, one summer night
Sat drowsing at his door. And mused, how grand
If all of this could last beyond a doubt—
This well-fed moon, this plump *Gemüthlichkeit;*
Pipe, breath, and summer never going out—
To vegetate through all eternity. . . .
But no such everlastingness for me!
God, if he can, keep me from such a blight.

> Death, it is but the long, cool night,
> And Life's a dull and sultry day.

It darkens; I grow drowsy;
I am weary of the light.

Over my bed a strange tree gleams
And there a nightingale is loud.
She sings of love, love only. . . .
I hear it, even in dreams.

My Mouche, the other day as I lay here,
Slightly propped up upon this mattress-grave
In which I've been interred these few eight years,
I saw a dog, a little pampered slave,
Running about and barking. I would have given
Heaven could I have been that dog; to thrive
Like him, so senseless—and so much alive!
And once I called myself a blithe Hellene,
Who am too much in love with life to live!
(The shrug is pure Hebraic) . . . For what I've been,
A lenient Lord will tax me—and forgive.
Dieu me pardonnera—c'est son métier.
But this is jesting. There are other scandals
You haven't heard. . . . Can it be dusk so soon?
Or is this deeper darkness? . . . Is that you,
Mother? How did you come? Where are the candles? . . .
Over my bed a strange tree gleams, half filled
With stars and birds, whose white notes glimmer through
Its seven branches now that all is stilled.
What? Friday night again and all my songs
Forgotten? Wait. . . . I still can sing—
Sh'ma Yisroel Adonai Elohenu,
Adonai Echod . . .
               Mouche! . . . Mathilde!

Nightmare by Day

There was no track
In the new snow.
Where could I go
Except go back
Where, row on row,
The trees stood black.

This, then, was peace.
Yet something said no.
Something below
The whispering trees
Made the warm flow
In my pulses freeze.

From where I stood,
Ten yards or so
Into the wood,
I watched it grow—
A trail of blood
Deep in the snow.

Nothing to show
Where it began.
No trace of man;
No other foe
More deadly than
One chuckling crow. . . .

What was this dream?
I do not know.
But still I seem
To wait for the blow,
And the red stream
Upon the snow.

On the Birth of a Child

Lo, to the battleground of life,
  Child, you have come, like a confident shout,
Out of a struggle—into strife;
  Out of a darkness—into doubt.

Girt with the fragile armor of youth,
  Child, you must ride into endless wars,
With the sword of protest, the buckler of truth,
  And a banner of love to sweep the stars.

About you the world's despair will surge;
  Into defeat you must plunge and grope.
Be to the faltering an urge;
  Be to the hopeless years a hope.

Be to the darkened world a flame;
  Be to its unconcern a blow.
For out of its pain and tumult you came,
  And into its tumult and pain you go.

On the Eve of New Wars

Man,
Do not despair;
You can surpass, with but a little care,
Nature's malevolent plan.

True,
The lion wreaks
His lust upon the lamb; talons and beaks
Sharpen on doves. But you,

Lord
Of earth and air,
Can flourish nonchalantly everywhere
Bomb, bayonet, gas and sword.

You,
Only you can find
A formula for killing your own kind
With a fine phrase or two.

Clear
A great path abroad.
Strike down your brother for the love of God.
Prove you are master here.

Poetry Reading: Women's Club

The poet stood reciting
　Examples of his art,
Considerately removing
　The veils about his heart.

Eager and self-revealing,
　He did his stripping well;
With every burning poem
　Another garment fell.

With passionate abandon
　He flung each line away;
Exulting in the pleasure
　Of noble self-display.

Until upon the platform
　Were piled his draperies.
And still the poet gestured,
　Naked and quite at ease.

And no one screamed or fainted;
　There was no stir or start.
The ladies all applauded
　Such a display of Art.

Portrait of a Child

Unconscious of amused and tolerant eyes,
He sits among his scattered dreams, and plays,
True to no one thing long; running for praise
With something less than half begun. He tries
To build his blocks against the furthest skies.
They fall; his soldiers tumble; but he stays
And plans and struts and laughs at fresh dismays,
Too confident and busy to be wise.

His toys are towns and temples; his commands
Bring forth vast armies trembling at his nod.
He shapes and shatters with impartial hands.
And, in his crude and tireless play, I see
The savage, the creator, and the god:
All that man was and all he hopes to be.

Portrait of a Dead Horse

Rotting it lay beneath the affable skies,
A fecund carrion, offering to the air
Its powerful benediction. Everywhere
About it sang a cloud of bright green flies.
Joyfully strengthened crows began to rise;
Great shining beetles ran, refreshed and fair;
And countless crawling things swarmed gladly there,
Called by the flesh that feeds and fortifies.

So, laughing, to that lively world he came:
Death, like a lover at some glorious task,
Free of all pain and pity, freed from strife.
His dark disguise could not conceal his aim;
For here, behind an ineffectual mask,
Sparkled the fresh and confident look of life.

Portrait of a Machine

What nudity is beautiful as this
Obedient monster purring at its toil;
These naked iron muscles dripping oil
And the sure-fingered rods that never miss.
This long and shining flank of metal is
Magic that greasy labor cannot spoil;
While this vast engine that could rend the soil
Conceals its fury with a gentle hiss.

It does not vent its loathing, does not turn
Upon its makers with destroying hate.
It bears a deeper malice; throbs to earn
Its master's bread and lives to see this great
Lord of the earth, who rules but cannot learn,
Become the slave of what his slaves create.

Portrait of a Nobody

There was the world that he had always found
In sleep, a heaven of long and lusty vices,
Where, swaggering in a hundred different guises,
He killed, he conquered, and was duly crowned.
And then there was the world where he was downed
By every small delay and hourly crisis;
A niggling world of customers and prices,
And reckoning the pennies to the pound.

Now who shall toll the bell for Jackson Kirk,
Who never lived his dream, nor here nor there.
Surely no demon warming to his work,
For Jackson nightly offered up his prayer.
And who on earth will ever heed a clerk,
Dangling 'twixt heaven and hell in pitiless air?

Portrait of a Poet

Fire he sings of, fierce and poignant flame;
Passion that bids a timid world be bold,
And Love that rides the tempest uncontrolled,
Scorning all customs with a greater claim.
Yet, underneath the ink, his soul is staid,
Calm, even calculating, shrewd and cold.
His pain lives but in print; his tears are rolled
And packed in small, neat lyrics for the trade.

He hawks his passions of assorted brands,
Romantic toys and tinsels of desire,
Marionettes that plead as he commands,
Rockets that sputter feebly, and expire.
And he is pleased and proud, and warms his hands
At the pale fireworks he takes for fire.

Portrait of a Pretty Woman

God, you complain, gave you a pretty face,
And that, you half imply, explains it all:
Your sudden rise and still more sudden fall;
The flashy triumph and half-proud disgrace.
Bitter, but still resolved to keep your place,
You mock at signs of faith and honor, call
Life an unmeaning farce, a madman's brawl,
And lay it all on Him, in any case.

But why blame God? Is it His fault again?
He knows, it seems, little of needs or goals.
God's a haphazard giver, and all men
Grow careless with their battered aureoles.
He made you with a pretty face. . . . But then,
God cannot make us all with pretty souls.

Portrait of a Sonnet Sequence

Here Rhetoric in tatters beats its breast,
And calls upon the bugles to intone
Pompous profundities that have been blown
By countless other trumpets long at rest.
Here Eloquence is an old actor dressed
In faded fustian on a tinsel throne,
Mouthing his syllables: "Thou . . . great . . . alone . . .
Vast . . . immemorial . . . beauty . . . unexpressed."

And while the sound disturbs indifferent air,
Invoking glamour in its grandiose moods,
The summoned spirit enters. Blare on blare
Ushers in Old Solemnity, while broods
Of hoary metaphors reveal him there
In patches torn from purple platitudes.

Portrait of the Rhetorician

Words are his last security. All else
Crumbles and rots. Man's loftiest stone is thrust
Into the patient and ironic dust.
Proud battleships and scornful citadels
Are tawdry playtoys, brittle iron shells
That go down in forgotten pools of rust.
But words, mere words, invulnerable, august,
Become his watchful soldier-sentinels.

He makes them do his fighting; sits and calls
On them to keep the world from going free.
They build him cozy nooks where he may be
Safe from the vulgar day's alarms and brawls;
While life, foiled by this soft persistency,
Beats futile hands on vague, invisible walls.

Prayer

God, though this life is but a wraith,
  Although we know not what we use,
Although we grope with little faith,
  Give me the heart to fight—and lose.

Ever insurgent let me be,
  Make me more daring than devout;
From sleek contentment keep me free,
  And fill me with a buoyant doubt.

Open my eyes to visions girt
  With beauty, and with wonder lit—
But let me always see the dirt,
  And all that spawn and die in it.

Open my ears to music; let
  Me thrill with Spring's first flutes and drums—
But never let me dare forget
  The bitter ballads of the slums.

From compromise and things half done,
  Keep me, with stern and stubborn pride;
And when, at last, the fight is won,
  God, keep me still unsatisfied.

Return to Birds

When cities prod me with demands
Of many minds and many hands,
When life becomes a cry of bargains
In unassimilated jargons,
And men bewilder men with words,
Suddenly I remember birds:
Goldfinches, those untamed canaries,
Preferring thistle-seed to cherries,
Shaking their broken crystal notes
Carelessly out of china throats.
Robin, the Spring's first feathered offering,
Whose burly strut is free of suffering
Except in drouth when his refrain
Echoes irascibly for rain.
Every bird on every hill
Whose small tongues twist and turn and trill:
The catbird, Nature's parodist,
In whose bright mill all sounds are grist—
Cluck, coloratura, mew and squawk.
The redstart's prattle, like the talk
Flung by pert brooks to tolerant stones,
Contentment strengthening their bones.
The ovenbird, pedantic creature,
Crying for "Teacher! Teacher! Teacher!"
The oriole, that childish bird,
Importunate to be seen and heard.
The cardinal, a crimson arrow.
The chestnut-crowned staccato sparrow
Whose voice is slivered in high chips.
The thrasher's frenzied sweeps and dips.
Dun city sparrows, numerous
As Jews and more ubiquitous,
Common to every slum and park.
Swallows, those arcs within an arc.
The hummingbird's arrested spark,
Half flame, half flower, blossoming where

Emerald and ruby burn in air.
The nighthawk's ghostly drum; the shrill
Insistence of the whip-poor-will.
The chebec, that small plague among
The flies with Egypt on its tongue.
Swifts, and their irrepressible young,
To whom all chimney homes are free.
Phoebes whose domesticity
Has no concern with privacy.
The purple martin's undramatic
Ecstasy of the acrobatic.
The blue jay, bully of the boughs,
Usurping any half-built house,
Comedian-brawler among leaves,
Roisterer, rascal, king of thieves.
The sentimental peewee's call,
Persuasive in its dying fall,
More languid than a pampered woman's.
The partridge ruffling out his summons.
Crow in his sheath of violet-jet,
A ravening scold in silhouette.
The kingbird with plume-shadowed crest,
Quirring defiance from his nest.
Fat bobolink, impetuous singer,
Who, living, is a lavish flinger
Of notes too prodigal for man,
And, dead, the gourmet's ortolan.
The yellowthroat's beseeching phrase,
Void of self-pity or self-praise.
That country questioner, the chat.
Wrens who have all the answers pat.
The tanager's abrupt rebellion,
Taunting the greenery with vermilion.
Field sparrow's mastery of change,
An opera in himself, whose range
His little measured breath lifts clear
Beyond the finest fleshly ear.
Metallic luster, grating cackle

That marks the iridescent grackle.
Those flakes of sky let loose, rose-breasted
Bodies lightly blueberry-dusted,
New England's liveliest muezzins,
The rusty robin's closest cousins.
Always a challenge, the unweary
Crescendo of the confident veery,
That thrush of overtones. And lush
As a long waterfall, the thrush
Himself, brown hermit of the trail,
Our lark, our more than nightingale,
Surpassing interval and scale. . . .

These are the happy ones; their breath
Is song, their element is faith.
Untouched by all the transient oddities
They do not traffic in commodities.
They neither kill for sport nor care
What way the wind will blow or where;
Their flight does not pollute the air;
Their mornings have no yesterdays,
Who, in themselves, have infinite ways
Of turning petulance to praise;
Who never trick themselves with words.
Gratefully I return to birds.

Roast Leviathan

"Old Jews!" Well, David, aren't we?
What news is that to make you see so red,
To swear and almost tear your beard in half?
Jeered at? Well, let them laugh.
You can laugh longer when you're dead.

It is the final Day.
A blast of Gabriel's horn has torn away
The last haze from our eyes, and we can see
Past the three hundred skies and gaze upon
The Ineffable Name engraved deep in the sun.
Now one by one, the pious and the just
Are seated by us, radiantly risen
From their dull prison in the dust.
And then the festival begins!
A sudden music spins great webs of sound,
Spanning the ground, the stars and their companions;
While, from the cliffs and canyons of blue air,
Prayers of all colors, cries of exultation
Rise into choruses of singing gold.
And, at the height of this bright consecration,
The whole Creation's rolled before us.
The seven burning heavens unfold.
We see the first (the only one we knew)
Dispersed and, shining through,
The other six declining: Those that hold
The stars and moons, together with all those
Containing rain, and fire, and sullen weather;
Cellars of dew-fall higher than the brim;
Huge arsenals with centuries of snows;
Infinite rows of storms, and swarms of seraphim.

Now comes our constantly increased reward.
The Lord commands that monstrous beast,
Leviathan, to be our feast.
What cheers ascend from horde on ravenous horde!

One hears the towering creature rend the seas,
Frustrated, cowering, and his pleas ignored.
In vain his great, belated tears are poured—
For this was he created, kept, and nursed.
Cries burst from all the millions that attend:
"Ascend, Leviathan, it is the end!
We hunger and we thirst! Ascend!"

Observe him first, my friend.

> God's deathless plaything rolls an eye
> Five hundred thousand cubits high.
> The smallest scale upon his tail
> Could hide six dolphins and a whale.
> His nostrils breathe, and on the spot
> The churning waves turn seething hot.
> If he be hungry, one huge fin
> Drives seven thousand fishes in;
> And when he drinks what he may need,
> The rivers of the earth recede.
> Yet he is more than huge and strong—
> Twelve brilliant colors play along
> His sides until, compared to him,
> The naked, burning sun seems dim.
> New scintillating rays extend
> Through endless singing space and rise
> Into an ecstasy that cries:
> "Ascend, Leviathan, ascend!"

God now commands the multicolored bands
Of angels to intrude and slay the beast,
That His good sons may have a feast of food.
But as they come, Leviathan sneezes twice.
And, numb with sudden pangs, each arm hangs slack.
Black terror seizes them; blood freezes into ice
And every angel flees from the attack.
God, with a look that spells eternal law,
Compels them back.

But though they fight, and smite him tail and jaw,
Nothing avails; upon his scales their swords
Break like frayed cords and, worse than blades of straw,
Bend towards the hilt, wilting like faded grass.
Defeat and fresh retreat. . . . But once again
God's murmurs pass among them and they mass
With firmer steps upon the crowded plain.
Vast clouds of spears and stones rise from the ground.
But every dart flies past and rocks rebound
To the disheartened angels falling around.

A pause.
The angel host withdraws
With empty boasts throughout its sullen files.
Suddenly God smiles.
On the walls of heaven a tumble of light is caught.
Low thunder rumbles like an afterthought;
And God's slow laughter calls:
"Behemot!"

    Behemot, sweating blood,
    Uses for his daily food
    All the fodder, flesh, and juice
    That twelve tall mountains can produce.

    Jordan, flooded to the brim,
    Is a single gulp to him;
    Two great streams from Paradise
    Cool his lips and scarce suffice.

    When he shifts from side to side
    Earthquakes gape and open wide;
    When a nightmare makes him snore,
    All the dead volcanoes roar.

    In the space between each toe,
    Kingdoms rise and saviours go;
    Epochs fall and causes die
    In the lifting of his eye.

Wars and justice, love and death,
These are but his wasted breath;
Chews a planet for his cud—
Behemot sweating blood.

Roused from his unconcern,
Behemot burns with anger.
Dripping sleep and languor from his heavy haunches,
He turns from deep disdain and launches
A mountain on the thickening air,
And with weird cries of sickening despair
Flies at Leviathan.
None can surmise the struggle that ensues.
The eyes lose sight of it, and words refuse
To tell the story in its gory might.
Night passes after night,
And still the fight continues, still the sparks
Fly from the iron sinews, till the marks
Of fire and belching thunder fill the dark
And, almost torn asunder, one falls stark,
Hammering upon the other!

What clamor now is born, what crashings rise!
Hot lightnings lash the skies and frightening cries
Clash with the hymns of saint and seraphim.
The bloody limbs thrash through a ruddy dusk,
Till one great tusk of Behemot has gored
Leviathan, restored to his full strength,
Who, dealing fiercer blows in those last throes,
Closes on reeling Behemot at length,
Piercing him with steel-pointed claws,
Straight through the jaws to his disjointed head.
And both lie dead.

Then come the angels!
With hoists and levers, joists and poles,
With knives and cleavers, ropes and saws,
Down the long slopes to the gaping maws,

The angels hasten; hacking and carving,
So nought will be lacking for the starving
Chosen of God, who in frozen wonderment
Realize now what the terrible thunder meant.
How their mouths water while they are looking
At miles of slaughter and sniffing the cooking!
Whiffs of delectable fragrance swim by;
Spice-laden vagrants that float and entice,
Tickling the throat and brimming the eye.
Ah! What rejoicing and crackling and roasting!
Ah! How the boys sing as, cackling and boasting,
The angels' old wives and their nervous assistants
Run in to serve us.
                                And while we are toasting
The Fairest of All, they call from the distance—
The rare ones of Time, they share our enjoyment;
Their only employment to bear jars of wine
And shine like the stars in a circle of glory. . . .

Peace without end.
Peace will descend on us, discord will cease;
And we, now so wretched, will lie stretched out,
Free of old doubt, on our cushions of ease.
And, a gold canopy over our bed,
The skin of Leviathan, tail-tip to head,
Soon will be spread till it covers the skies.
Light will still rise from it; millions of bright
Facets of brilliance, shaming the white
Glass of the moon, inflaming the night.

So Time shall pass, and rest, and pass again,
Burn with an endless zest and then return,
Walk at our side and tide us to new joys;
God's voice to guide us, beauty as our staff.
Thus shall Life be when Death has disappeared. . . .

Jeered at? Well, let them laugh.

Sardonic Moon

What cold, celestial laughter
  Disturbs me in the night?
It is the moon that enters
  The street with a ripple of light.

His ghostly mirth reminds me
  How well I ought to know
That flash of evil humor
  Revealed some months ago.

Upon a beach where the pattering
  Waves were music enough,
Two lovers walked, believing
  The world was made for their love.

The stars, the crooning silence
  Worked through their stammering lips;
Slowly it drew them together
  Like rudderless, driven ships.

In the deserted pavilion
  They clung with a passionate faith;
Hurling, as though for the first time,
  The deathless challenge to death.

And then, old moon, I saw you.
  Your sharp and cynical smile
Cut through our boasts and bravados,
  Breaking them off for a while.

Your long, ironic glances
  Mocked us and seemed to inquire
What ash would be left tomorrow
  Of this brief spasm of fire?

We paused. And then, for an answer,
  She laughed in my arms and said,
"Why should the living listen
  To you, the impotent dead!"

Scarcely Spring

Nothing is real. The world has lost its edges;
The sky, uncovered, is the one thing clear.
The earth is little more than atmosphere
Where yesterday were rocks and naked ridges.
Nothing is fixed. Tentative rain dislodges
Green upon green or lifts a coral spear
That breaks in blossom, and the hills appear
Too frail to be the stony fruit of ages.

Nothing will keep. Even the heavens waver.
Young larks, whose first thought is to cry aloud,
Have spent their bubble notes. And here or there
A few slow-hearted boys and girls discover
A moon as insubstantial as a cloud
Painted by air on washed and watery air.

Short Sonnet: November

This is an avenue of gold
Impervious to rain and rust,
Where sunlight is a yellow dust
Too fine for all but leaves to hold.
When even the rocks return to mold,
These will resist Time's gradual thrust.
So we declared. And then a gust
From some far world blew suddenly cold.

The gold that powdered every tree
Was lightly loosened, flake by flake.
We watched the wind's sharp fingers take
Leaf after leaf deliberately.
Murder was out; death was awake.
There was no more we cared to see.

Shylock, Christian
(THE MERCHANT OF VENICE, ACT VI)

Enter SHYLOCK *and* TUBAL

SHYLOCK:

Isaac's a robber, there's an end to it.
Three thousand ducats! Does the man believe
I cannot tell a flawed and yellow bastard
From one of royal blood?—I mean the diamond.
By Aaron's rod! I'll trim, I'll tutor him!
I know his bag of miserable tricks
Filched from his father. That old patriarch,
His reverend father, *selig*, used to say,
"Whenever a person asks for carat diamonds
Show him the melee first. No salesman's needed
To sell a man the thing he wants." These Jews!
These Jews! Put not your trust in one of them!

TUBAL:

Shylock, those notes are false as they are new.
There was a time you sang a different song.

SHYLOCK:

Pst! In your ear. The tune is popular,
And I have learned to whistle it by heart.
Look you, six years ago I was the butt
Of Christian Venice, jeered and spat upon.
Pert fools with painted faces followed me
To mock and rip my Jewish gabardine.
Who were my enemies? Antonio,
Bassanio, and other merchant-wasters?
They were the least. My enemy was the state,
With legal crime, precise chicanery,
And all its smooth machinery of hate.
What was my trial? A mock, a gaudy farce;

All Venice held its sides for seven weeks
When the news trickled through familiar leaks
How Portia, in a travesty of law,
Ruled that a pound of flesh includes no blood—
Suppose your butcher were to tell you that!—
And, merriest jest of all, the Court upheld her!
My goods were forfeit—half of them, at least—
Seized by the state, mark you, the sovereign state;
And, as a crowning stroke of charity,
I was allowed to eat the flesh of swine
And plunge my fingers into blood-pudding.
Meanwhile, the Duke and the Magnificos
Approved the sentence with unblinking eyes,
While back of them the effigy of Justice
(The Lord knows how!) maintained its gravity.

TUBAL:

So, out of fear, you made yourself a Christian!

SHYLOCK:

Pronounce the word with not so great a scorn.
By Balaam's ass, we Christians, too, are human.
Has not a Christian eyes, hands, properties?
Can he not feel the goad and stab of life
Almost the same as the less favored races?
Does he not eat and drink and copulate
Casually like the other animals?
Does he not humbly pray to God for what
His neighbor has—and, eager to help the Lord,
First help himself as earnest of his faith?
Does he not show himself upon the peak
Of all that's civilized by playing cards,
Drinking his wits away, fouling his home,
Letting his lusts bring him to any bed?
And, by our Lady—meaning whom it may—
Is he not crowned of all, the king of commerce,
The golden rock on which the state is founded?

89

Oh, what a tradesman he can be! You Jews
Are shoestring mendicants compared to him.
His world is business. Business is his hearth,
His crowded stage, his school, his synagogue.
He bloats his industries with surplus wares,
Then makes a war to find an outlet for them.
No trivial bargaining, no petty feuds
Divert his thoughts; his mind is grandiose
With wholesale hatreds, huge and thriving death.
I tell you, and it is my purse that speaks,
Turn Christian, Tubal, you will profit by it.

TUBAL:

Turn Christian!

SHYLOCK:

      Why not? There speaks prejudice.
Observe and judge what it has done for me.
"There's more rejoicing"— But you know the text. . . .
And so the erstwhile sinner, so old Shylock
Is now an ornament of the republic.
Antonio is my friend and, what is more,
The private partner of my enterprise—
We have a diamond-cutting branch in Amsterdam.
Now that I am a pillar of the church,
Antonio's not averse to share the fruits
Of trees I pruned in my apprenticeship—
I mean the training of my Jewish years.
And so my world has honey on its tongue
Brewed, by a miracle, from vinegar.
Jessica's back. She left the fool she married,
A primping thistledown, within a year,
And now she keeps my books, mine more than ever.
I am the city's freedom and its voice.
When, in the name of trade, I call for Law,
It is the Law that, thundering, speaks for me!
They flock to me for crumbs on the Rialto;

Even Gratiano, with an eye to ducats,
Preens his best phrases, hoping for a hint
By which an honest thief might benefit.
And I am made to feel I am their equal!
Because, by Solomon, these merchants think
That, being one of them, I have forgotten
My pride, which is both refuge and rebellion,
Everything but the passion to possess;
Crying, like them, "My Gold! My God! My Gold!"
Slaying each other for a pennyweight.
Thus, clutching at their loot, I've seen them die,
Their fingers drenched in Christian blood, the cry
Of Progress and Religion on their lips.

O father Abraham, what we Christians are!

                                        (*Exeunt*)

Sic Semper—

Down—down he came,
Burning his soul with the exploring flame.

Kingship among the angels lost, honor in Heaven forsaking
For earth's awaking.

He, the Light-Bringer, Fire-Scatterer, plunging through death in
    the dark
With his one spark

Torn from the bright
Heart of Intelligence whose least universe is Light,

So that the clod
Might lift itself, light-shielded and light-shod,
And man grow like his God.

A snare
Of winds tore the bare hands and throat, froze the fine hair,
Whipped him with knives of air.

But down—down he flew,
Nor rested till the burning seeds were planted and the dark mind
    knew
Wisdom defining one and two,
False from true.

Then man—aware too well
What truth would cost, what love and wisdom would compel—
Put Lucifer in hell.

Sinfonia Domestica

His eyes grow hot, his words grow wild;
    He swears to break the mold and leave her.
She smiles at him as at a child
    That's touched with fever.

She smoothes his ruffled wings, she leans
    To comfort, pamper, and restore him;
And when he sulks or scowls, she preens
    His feathers for him.

He hungers after stale regrets,
    Nourished by what she offers gaily;
And all he thinks he never gets
    She feeds him daily.

He lusts for freedom; cries how long
    Must he be bound by what controlled him.
Yet he is glad the chains are strong,
    And that they hold him.

She knows he feels all this, but she
    Is far too wise to let him know it;
He needs to nurse the agony
    That suits a poet.

He laughs to see her shape his life,
    As she half coaxes, half commands him;
And groans it's hard to have a wife
    Who understands him.

Six Epigrams

On a Politician   *After Hearing the Whip-poor-will*
> Loud laureate of nought, go play
> Thy steam-calliope to frogs and 'fright 'em,
> Thou who hast never anything to say,
> And sayest it with force, *ad infinitum.*

On a Poet
> She counts her world well lost for whom
> A wisecrack is the Crack of Doom.
> She gags as neatly as she grieves,
> And wears her heart out—on both sleeves.

On a Popularizer
> Midwife to all the Muses, you grow rich
> By making the immortal less divine.
> With what finesse you trim, and cut, and stitch,
> Feigning that every stitch—in time—serves Nine.

On a Supreme Court Judge
> How well this figure represents the Law:
>   This pose of neuter justice, sterile cant;
> This Roman Emperor with an iron jaw,
>   Wrapped in the black silk of a maiden aunt.

On a Feeble Whistler
"Seated by the roadside I shall wait for America to catch up."
—G. S. VIERECK

> What though the crowd, with laudable defection
> Has gone in quite the opposite direction,
> His feeble penny-whistle demonstrates
> It serves him right who only sits and waits.

On a Self-made Philosopher

"Life was my university,"
He boasts, and waits for approbation;
Revealing, to the nth degree,
The sad results of education.

Song Tournament: New Style

Rain, said the first, as it falls in Venice
Is like the dropping of golden pennies
Into a sea as smooth and bright
As a bowl of curdled malachite.

Storm, sang the next, in the streets of Peking
Is like the ghost of a yellow sea-king,
Scooping the dust to find if he may
Discover what earth has hidden away.

The rush of Spring, smiled the third, in Florence
Is wave upon wave of laughing torrents,
A flood of birds, a water-voiced calling,
A green rain rising instead of falling.

The wind, cried the fourth, in the Bay of Naples
Is a quarrel of leaves among the maples,
A war of sunbeams idly fanned,
A whisper softer than sand on sand.

Then spoke the last: God's endless tears,
Too great for Heaven, anoint the spheres,
While every drop becomes a well
In the fathomless, thirsting heart of Hell.

And thus five bards, who could boast of travel
Fifty miles from their native gravel,
Rose in the sunlight and offered their stanzas
At the shrine of the Poetry Contest in Kansas.

"So Rein und Schön" (WITH A VOLUME OF HEINE)

Like some young flower, cool and white,
  With the stars' kiss still on its brow,
You shine through my heart's dusk, and light
  The dark concern that gathers now.

Half on my lips, a fearful hope
  Starts like a prayer already planned;
Toward your bright head my fingers grope,
  But something holds my hand.

Prayers are not what you want. I see
  That, when all other beauty fails,
You will not alter, you will be
  As fair and young—and hard as nails.

Still Life

A bowl of fruit upon a piece of silk:
Stiff pears and awkward apples, with the leaves
A querulous and contradictory green.
Harsh reds and surly yellows, bitter blacks,
Savagely massed with strong and angry skill—
A canvas rioting with love and hate.

Never have I beheld such fierce contempt,
Nor heard a voice so full of vehement life
As this that shouted from a bowl of fruit,
High-pitched, malignant, agonized and clear.

I never knew the man that did this thing,
This piece of life too urgent to be still,
And yet I know him better than I know myself.

Summer Storm

We lay together in the sultry night.
A feeble light
From some invisible street-lamp crept
Into the corner where you slept,
Fingered your cheeks, flew softly round your hair,
Then dipped in the sweet valley of your breasts
And fluttered, like a bird between two nests,
Till it lay quiet there.
My eyes were closing and I may have dreamed—
At least it seemed
That you and I
Had ceased to be but were somehow
As earth and sky. . . .

The night grew closer still, and now
Heat-lightnings played between us, and warm thrills
Ran through the cool sides of the trembling hills.
Then darkness and a tension in the black
Hush like a breath held back;
A rippling through the ground, a windless breeze
That reached down to the sensitive roots of trees;
A tremor like the pulse of muffled knocks,
Or like the silent opening of locks.
There was a rising of unfettered seas
With great tides pulling at the stars and rocks
As though to draw them all together.
Then in a burst of blinding weather,
The lightnings flung
Long, passionate arms about the earth that clung
To her wild lover.
Suddenly above her
The whole sky tumbled in a sweeping blaze,
Gathering earth in one tight-locked embrace,
Drenching her in a flood of silver flame.
Hot thunders came;
And still the storm kept plunging, seeking ever

The furthest cranny, till the faraway
Streams felt each penetrating quiver
And the most hidden river
Rose and became released.

At last the stabbings ceased,
The thunders died.
But still they lay
Side by side,
While moonbeams crept
Into the heavenly corner where earth slept;
Dipping among her rosy hills, lighting above
Her curved and sloping hollows, till
She too was still.
Beloved and blest,
His cloudy head lay, seeking rest
In the sweet-smelling valley of her breast,
And each was huddled in each other's love—
Or so it seemed.
My eyes were closing and I may have dreamed.

Swimmers

I took the crazy short-cut to the bay;
Over a fence or two and through a hedge,
Jumping a private road, along the edge
Of backyards full of drying wash it lay.
And now, the last set being played and over,
I hurried past the ruddy lakes of clover;
I swung my racket at astonished oaks,
My arm still tingling from aggressive strokes.
Tennis was over for the day—
I took the leaping short-cut to the bay.

Then the quick plunge into the cool, green dark,
The windy waters rushing past me, through me;
Filled with a sense of some heroic lark
Existing in a vigor clean and roomy.
Swiftly I rose to meet the cat-like sea
That sprang upon me with a hundred claws,
And grappled, pulled me down and played with me.
Then, held suspended in the tightening pause
When one wave grows into a toppling acre,
I dived headlong into the foremost breaker,
Pitting against a cold and turbulent strife
The feverish intensity of life.
Out of the foam I lurched and rode the wave,
Swimming, hand over hand, against the wind;
I felt the sea's vain pounding, and I grinned
Knowing I was its master, not its slave.

Back on the curving beach I stood again,
Facing the bath-house, when a group of men,
Stumbling beneath some sort of weight, went by.
I could not see the heavy thing they carried;
I only heard: "He never gave a cry—"
"Who's going to tell her?" "Yes, and they just married—"
"Such a good swimmer, too . . ." And then they passed,
Leaving the silence throbbing and aghast.

A moment there my frightened heart hung slack,
And then the rich, retarded blood came back
Singing a livelier tune; and in my pulse
Beat the great wave that endlessly exults.
Why I was there and whither I must go,
I did not care. Enough for me to know
The same persistent struggle and the glowing
Waste of all spendthrift hours, bravely showing
Life, an adventure perilous and gay,
And death, a long and vivid holiday.

Ten Years Old

A city child, rooms are to him no mere
Places to live in. Each one has a clear
Color and character of its own. His toys
And tumbled books make the small bedroom seem
The place to build a practicable dream.
He likes the brilliant parlor and enjoys
Nothing so much as bringing other boys
To romp among the delicate furniture,
And brush within an inch of ivories, lamps,
And other things not held by iron clamps,
Like Chinese vases, neatly insecure.
He views the kitchen with a hungry eye
And loafs about it, nibbling at the stray
Dry crumbs of gossip that may drop his way,
Standing so innocently inattentive. Sly,
And with a squirrel's curiosity,
Careless of barred or sacred corners, he
Hunts back of shelves until he finds the key
With which to open bureau drawers and pry
Into forbidden desks and cupboards; there
Are scores of mysteries forbidden, new,
And so well hidden, they need looking through.
But most of all he likes the bathroom where
The panel mirror shows his four feet two;
Where, with a towel or bathrobe, he can strike
A hundred attitudes not only like
His printed heroes but the gods themselves.
Stripping himself, he dreams and dances there,
The pink embodiment of Peter Pan.
Or, changing to an older superman,
He turns to Siegfried brandishing his sword
And Jason snatching at the Golden Fleece.
The figures crowd around him and increase:
Now he is David battling for the Lord,
Mixing his battle cries with psalms of peace.

Now he is Mowgli, at the cobra's hoard
With black Bagheera. Swiftly he has drawn
Excalibur from its invisible sheath.
He is Ulysses on his native heath,
Tristram, Tom Sawyer, and Bellerophon;
Cadmus about to sow the dragon's teeth;
The shining Parsifal who knew no sin;
Sir Launcelot and Huckleberry Finn;
George Washington, and Captain Hook, and Thor;
Hänsel awaking in the magic wood;
Frank Merriwell, John Silver, Robin Hood—
He is all these and half a hundred more.
He scowls and strides, he utters harsh commands.
Great armies follow him to newborn lands
Battling for treasures lost or glories gone.
None can withstand the thunder of his frown.
His eye is terrible; the walls go down.
Cries of the conquered mingle with the cheers,
While through the clash and battle smoke he hears—
"Richard! Get through! And put your stockings on!"

The Dark Chamber

The brain forgets but the blood will remember.
　There, when the play of sense is over,
The last, low spark in the darkest chamber
　Will hold all there is of love and lover.

The war of words, the life-long quarrel
　Of self against self will resolve into nothing;
Less than the chain of berry-red coral
　Crying against the dead black of her clothing.

What has the brain that it hopes to last longer?
　The blood will take from forgotten violence
The groping, the break of her voice in anger.
　There will be left only color and silence.

These will remain, these will go searching
　Your veins for life when the flame of life smolders:
The night that you two saw the mountains marching
　Up against dawn with the stars on their shoulders;

The jetting poplars' arrested fountains
　As you drew her under them, easing her pain;
The notes, not the words, of a half-finished sentence;
　The music, the silence. . . . These will remain.

The Dream and the Blood

Go back, dark blood, to the springs from which you came.
  Go back, though each mutinous drop swells upward in flood.
What! Am I nothing more now than a wave of onrushing flame?
  Nothing but sport of my pulse? Back, back, dark blood!

Am I not master here in my own house of flesh?
  Cease roaring and rising. Be still, I tell you, be still.
I have work that calls for cool evenings; I have stuff of the mind
    to thresh.
  Must you pit your unreasoning hunger against my determinate
    will?

I tell you this body for which we are always contending
  Is more than mere fuel for you to be turned into ash.
It was shaped by white visions of leaving its bones, of extending
  Itself into realms where your heat would be less than a flash.

What! Will you not even listen? I hear you, O hater
  Of all that I plan. I hear how the thud
In my veins beats your victory. . . . Later, then, later;
  Give me myself for an hour. Go back, dark blood.

The Leaf

"Stay here tonight—this one night, mother.
  I dread to lie alone.
The bed is hard as a bed of granite;
  The pillow is like a stone."

"Surely I'll stay. But your nightmare's over.
  Keep covered; the air is raw.
'Twas something, child, you heard in the forest,
  Or something you saw."

"The nightmare's done, but it won't be over.
  There's never an end to grief.
Yes, it was something I saw in the forest.
  I saw a blood-red leaf."

"A blood-red leaf? But the month is August.
  The maples are solid green.
The death of the year in the prime of summer
  No man has seen."

"No man, perhaps, but a woman might have;
  Or a flower that's burst its bud.
And as for the color, a frost may have done it—
  Or the dropping of blood."

"Lie down and close your eyes, my darling;
  Lie down as a daughter should.
You frighten yourself with these foolish fancies.
  There's nothing wild in our wood."

"Nothing wilder than I am, mother;
  Nothing, as you will see.
Nothing except the flood of lightnings
  As I held him under the tree.

"But never again will that thunder shake me,
　　And no one will quiet his cries.
No girl will cradle a head that's matted,
　　Nor lift him the way he lies.

"So free was he with life, mother,
　　He filled it over the brim.
Yet now he lies more quietly
　　Than the red leaves under him.

"Stay here this night, for there'll be no other;
　　There'll be no names to misname.
He'll have no child, as you have, to curse him,
　　And I'll have no body to blame."

The Scraping of a Scythe

The bird was blue as he was blithe;
　　His pleasure brought the sky around.
And then the scraping of a scythe
　　Let fall its rusty flakes of sound.

Two voices tried the air. The one
　　Still pulled its half of heaven to earth;
The other, desperate to be done,
　　Rose on a note of grinding mirth.

Cold caught the day and shook it through.
　　I did not need to hear the words
To know what had transpired; I knew
　　The note that menaced more than birds.

Our fields, uncut, are never clear
　　Of knotted grass and tangled withe.
But there is peace. I shall not hear
　　The bitter scraping of a scythe.

The Stone's Hymn

Earthquakes prepared me, made my bed;
    Worlds rose within me, fell apart.
Now small lives move beneath and overhead,
    While unseen heavens open in my heart.

Beyond extremities of pain,
    I touch the very source of might.
Do I not drink the warm, impersonal rain,
    Feed on the lavish and indifferent light?

Here, in a permanent peace, I lie
    Till finity and all its shapes are done;
And sorrow is an air that passes by,
    And death a little absence of the sun.

Content to wait while kingdoms crack,
    And men conspire and planets climb,
I know no fear, no weariness, no lack,
    Who have eternity instead of time.

The Wanderer

Is it a tribute or betrayal when,
    Turning from all the sweet, accustomed ways,
I leave your lips and eyes to seek you in
        Some other face?

Why am I searching after what I have?
    And going far to find the near at hand?
I do not know. I only know I crave
        To find you at the end.

I only know that love has many a hearth;
    That hunger has an endless path to roam;
That beauty is the ghost that haunts the earth
        And leads me home.

The Woodpecker

In the world there were but two—
    She the sleeper, I the waker—
When upon our roof there flew
    An imperative woodpecker.

"What is that and who is there?"
    Cried my doubly dearest, waking.
"We are far and guests are rare
    And no stranger comes a-knocking."

Then I answered, "It may well
    Be the day of doom that wants us,
And perhaps it's Gabriel
    Making up an early census."

Then she laughed, "Belovèd, say,
    If he asks, I am not ready."
And the summoner flew away,
    And sleep took my tired lady.

I slept, too, though I could see
    A smaller house, a larger acre,
Where, one morning, we would be:
    I the sleeper, she the waker.

The Young Mystic

We sat together close and warm,
  My little tired boy and I,
  Watching across the evening sky
The coming of the storm.

No rumblings rose, no thunders crashed,
  The west wind scarcely sang aloud;
  But from a huge and solid cloud
The summer lightning flashed.

And then he whispered, "Father, watch;
  I think God's going to light His moon—"
  "And when, my boy?" "Oh, very soon.
I saw Him strike a match!"

Tired Gentleman

The train devours time; the storm
  Falls back before its headlong thrust.
Paper in hand, secure and warm,
  I skim the cream of loot and lust.

War is abroad; monsters obscene
  Shatter the sky. Upon the pane
I watch the world float by between
  The silver tadpoles of the rain.

My house has stood a hundred years,
  And it will stand a hundred more.
What is this folly that one hears?
  The mob is roaring? Let it roar.

There's naught to gain and much to lose,
  And rain has such a comforting sweep.
O rich content. I shut the news.
  I fold my hands, and go to sleep.

To a Vine-clad Telegraph Pole

You should be done with blossoming by now.
Yet here are leaves closer than any bough
That welcomes ivy. True, you were a tree
And stood with others in a marching line,
Less regular than this, of spruce and pine
And boasted branches rather than a trunk.
This is your final winter, all arms shrunk
To one crossbar bearing, haphazardly,
Four rusty strands. You cannot hope to feel
The electric sap run through those veins of steel.

The birds know this; the birds have hoodwinked you,
Crowding about you as they used to do.
The rainy robins huddled on your wire
And those black birds with shoulders dipped in fire
Have made you dream these vines; these tendrils are
A last despair in green, familiar
To derelicts of earth as well as sea.
Do not believe them, there is mockery
In their cool little jets of song. They know
What everyone but you learned long ago:
The stream of stories humming through your head
Is not your own. You dream. But you are dead.

To a Weeping Willow

You hypocrite!
You sly deceiver!
I have watched you fold your hands and sit
With your head bowed the slightest bit,
And your body bending and swaying
As though you were praying,
Like a devout and rapt believer.
You knew that folks were looking and you were
Well pleased with the effect of it:
Your over-mournful mien;
Your meek and almost languid stir;
Your widow's weeds of trailing green.
Wearing a grief in resignation clad,
You seemed so chastely, delicately sad.

You bold, young hypocrite—
I know you now!
Last night when every light was out,
I saw you wave one beckoning bough
And, with a swift and passionate shout,
The storm sprang up—and you, you exquisite,
You laughed a welcome to that savage lout.
I heard that thunder of his heavy boots.
And then in that dark, rushing weather,
You clung together;
Safe with your secret in the night's great cover,
You and your lover.
I saw his windy fingers in your hair;
I saw you tremble and try to tear
Free from your roots
In a headlong rush to him.
His face was dim.
But I could hear his kisses in the rain,
And I could see your arms clasp and unclasp.
His rough, impetuous grasp

Shook you and you let fall
Your torn and futile weeds, or flung them all
Joyfully in the air,
As if they were
Triumphant flags, to sing above
The stark and shameless victory of love!

Two Funerals

Upon a field of shrieking red
 A mighty general stormed and fell.
They raised him from the common dead
 And all the people mourned him well.
"Swiftly," they cried, "let honors come,
 And Glory with her deathless bays;
For him let every valiant drum
 And grieving bugle thrill with praise.
Has he not made the whole world fear
 The very lifting of his sword—
Has he not slain his thousands here
 To glorify Law and the Lord!
Then make his bed of sacred sod;
 To greater heights no man can win."
And each amused and ancient god
  Began to grin.

Facing a cold and sneering sky,
 Cold as the sneering hearts of men,
A man began to prophesy,
 To speak of love and faith again.
Boldly he spoke, and bravely dared
 The cruel word, the kindlier stone;
The armies mocked at him; he fared
 To battle gaily—and alone.
Alone he fought; alone, to move
 A world whose wars would never cease,
And all his blows were struck for love,
 And all his fighting was for peace.
They tortured him with thorns and rods,
 They hanged him on a frowning hill—
And all the old and heartless gods
  Are laughing still.

Upon Washington Bridge

Wordsworth, thou should'st be living in this, our
Victory over reason, life, and laws;
Daily the air with strictly timed applause
Expands in rumors of increasing power.
Rhetoric blooms, the world's perennial flower;
Raising a road-hymn to the latest cause,
We feed on platitudes and build with straws
Something we dream may be an ivory tower.

It is a beauteous evening; calm and free
We wash our minds of thought. Serenely clear
The lights upon the Palisades appear
To say the time is seven fifty-three.
Once more at peace, we go back home and hear
The Voice of God on Station XYZ.

Words for a Jig
(TO BE DANCED ON THE GRAVE OF AN ENEMY)

Thus I pay the visit
  Promised years ago.
Tell me, oh my friend, how is it
  There below?

Do these weeds and mullein
  Choke each angry mood,
Or increase your hard and sullen
  Torpitude?

You who sought distractions
  Howsoever base,
Have you learned to love inaction's
  Slower pace?

Here, at least, you've found that
  You belong to earth;
Dying on the careless ground that
  Gave you birth.

Do not let it fret you;
  Things are not so drear.
Though the heartless world forget you,
  I am here!

I have not forgotten
  How you loved the stir;
Black at heart and doubly rotten
  Though you are.

So I take my fiddle,
  And I roar a stave;
Dancing gaily on the middle
  Of your grave.

Such regard must cheer you
    In your misery,
Although I can scarcely hear you
    Thanking me.

But I ask no hands in
    Thanks or loud applause;
I am glad to sing and dance in
    Such a cause.

Thus I pay the visit
    Promised years ago.
Tell me, oh my friend, how is it
    There below?

Yes and No

Yes
Is made to bless
With natural largesse.

Yes is full sun;
Day well-begun,
And labor done;

The high
Response of the belovèd eye;
Approving sky;

Rich laughter; open hands;
The ripe expanse
Of casual circumstance.

Yes
Is no less
Than God's excess.

No
Is the slow
Finality of snow;
The soft blow deadening all that grow;

Locked brain;
The tight-lipped tugging at the rein;
The blood stopped in the vein;

Dull dying without death;
Lost faith
Sick of its own breath.

No is the freezing look,
The closed book,
The dream forsook.